OREGON

in words and pictures

BY DENNIS B. FRADIN

ILLUSTRATIONS BY RICHARD WAHL

MAPS BY LEN W. MEENTS

Consultant:
  Lynda C. Falkenstein, Professor
  Director, Law-Related Education
  Portland State University

CHILDRENS PRESS, CHICAGO

Ocean spray on the Oregon coast

Library of Congress Cataloging in Publication Data

Fradin, Dennis B
  Oregon in words and pictures.

  SUMMARY: Presents a brief history and description
of the Beaver State.
  1. Oregon—Juvenile literature. [1. Oregon]
I. Wahl, Richard, 1939-   II. Meents, Len W.
III. Title.
F876.3.F7   979.5   80-15183
ISBN 0-516-03937-7

Picture Acknowledgments:
SMITH-WESTERN INC., PORTLAND—Cover, pages, 2, 4, 31, 32, 37, 39, 41
TRAVEL INFORMATION, OREGON STATE HIGHWAY DIVISION—pages 6,
8, 11, 12, 15, 16, 19, 27, 28, 30
GILCREASE INSTITUTE—page 21
WEYERHAEUSER COMPANY—page 23
UNITED STATES DEPARTMENT OF THE INTERIOR, BUREAU OF
RECLAMATION—page 25
GAF CORPORATION—pages 35, 40
COVER—Wizard Island in Crater Lake

Oregon (OHR • ih • gahn) is one of our most beautiful states. The Pacific Ocean lies against its western shore. Rivers cut through mountains. They rush to the ocean. The state has snow-covered mountains two miles high. It has vast forests. Many animals live in the state.

Oregon's history is closely tied to these natural treasures. Indians made canoes from trees. They fished in salmon-filled streams. Later, fur trappers came to Oregon for beaver furs. In recent years, houses and wood products have been built from Oregon lumber. Oregon is the leading lumber-producing state. Oregon has much more.

Where is the deepest lake in the United States?
Where did wagon trains arrive after a 2,000-mile trip?
Where do fish climb ladders?

As you will learn, the answer to these questions is:
Oregon!

Rocks and bones show scientists what the land was like long ago. Sharks' teeth have been found on land that is now dry. Crocodile bones have been found, too. Millions of years ago, Oregon was covered by shallow seas.

For millions of years the land went through violent changes. Volcanoes exploded. One of these was Mount Mazama. Its top caved in. The hole that was left filled with water. This is how Crater Lake was formed. It is the deepest lake in the United States.

Winter wildlife at Crater Lake

Before there were people in Oregon, interesting animals lived there. There were mammoths and mastodons. They looked like big, furry elephants. There were saber-toothed tigers. Small horses ran about. There were even tiny camels.

The first people arrived in Oregon at least 10,000 years ago. They lived in caves. Their stone weapons have been found in caves and burial mounds. Paintings they made on cliffs can still be seen today.

In more recent times, many tribes of Indians lived in Oregon. Some of the tribes were the Chinook (shi • NOOK), Nez Percé (NEHZ PURSE), Bannock (BAN • uhk), and Modoc (MOH • dahk).

A modern-day Indian girl at the Pendleton Roundup

In the east, Indians used earth to make their houses. In the west there were more trees. There wooden houses were built.

Indians who lived near rivers fished. They used tough grasses to make fishnets. Then they caught salmon.

The Indians of Oregon used cedar trees to make long canoes. They also used wood to make bows and arrows. The Indians hunted deer, elk, and bears. They ate the meat. They used the skins to make clothes.

The Indians believed that animals had spirits. Some thought that their people were descended from bears. They called bears "Grandfather." Others believed that the coyote (kye • OH • tee) god created the Indians.

Spanish explorers were the first non-Indians in Oregon. Spain controlled Mexico (MECKS • ih • koh), far south of Oregon. Bartolome Ferrelo (bahr • TOH • loh • may feh • RAY • yoh) is thought to have explored the Oregon coast in 1543.

English explorer Sir Francis Drake is thought to have sailed into Oregon waters in 1579. Almost 200 years later, in 1778, Englishman James Cook sailed up the Oregon coast.

Americans entered the area soon afterward. In 1788 American Robert Gray arrived in his ship. It was named the *Columbia* (koh • LUM • bee • yah). In 1792 he sailed into a river. He named it the Columbia after his ship. Gray traded with the Indians for salmon and furs.

A mural in the Oregon state capitol pictures explorers Lewis and Clark.

In 1805 American explorers Meriwether Lewis and William Clark arrived in Oregon. They were tired after a long journey. Nez Percé Indians fed them and cared for them. Lewis and Clark then traveled by canoe on the Columbia River. They reached the Pacific Ocean. Lewis and Clark told President Thomas Jefferson that Oregon was rich in animal furs.

Furs brought white people into Oregon. At this time, millions of beavers lived in Oregon rivers. Sea otters swam in the waters of the Pacific coast. Deer, elk, and bears roamed through the forests. Many people wanted clothes made from these animal furs. The furs were very valuable. A single sea otter fur was known to sell for as much as $2,500 in those days.

English and American fur traders arrived. They gave pots, mirrors, and trinkets to the Indians. In return they received bundles of the animal furs. Fur trappers caught the animals themselves. There were so many beavers that fifty a day could be killed easily. Sea otters were also plentiful. They are friendly animals. They like to float on their backs while eating clams. It was easy to kill them.

In the early 1800s many American ships arrived to trade for furs. American fur trader John Jacob Astor arrived. He built a large fur-trading post in Oregon. It was called Astoria (ass • TORE • ee • uh). Astoria was the first non-Indian settlement in Oregon. Today it is the state's oldest town.

The United States and England made an agreement. They decided that both countries could trade for furs in Oregon. English fur-trading was run by Dr. John McLoughlin (mick • LOFF • lihn). He was a tall man. He had white hair and a white beard. McLoughlin became ruler of the Oregon area for more than twenty years. He kept peace with the Indians. He helped people who wanted to set up farms in the area. He helped set up sawmills to cut wood. McLoughlin helped the English make millions of dollars in the fur business. English and American people thought of McLoughlin as their leader. He is now remembered as the "Father of Oregon."

The John McLoughlin House in Oregon City, a town he founded

In 1836 Dr. Marcus Whitman took a wagon over a new trail into the Oregon area. Dr. Whitman was an American *missionary* (MISH • un • air • ee). His job was to teach the Indians about Christianity (kris • tchee • YAN • ih • tee). He wanted them to become Christians.

State capitol mural of a wagon train on the Oregon Trail

The trail Dr. Whitman took became known as the Oregon Trail. People in the eastern United States heard about Oregon. They heard that there was good farmland in the state. They began to go there. They traveled on the Oregon Trail. In 1843 about 1,000 people took the Oregon Trail. Every year, more and more Americans arrived in Oregon.

The beginning of the Oregon Trail was in Independence, Missouri (mih • ZOO • ree). That was about 2,000 miles from Oregon. People gathered there in covered wagons. They fit everything they could into their wagons. Many wagons made a "wagon train." The trip west was very hard. The people had to find places where rivers could be crossed. They had to find fresh drinking water. On the way they tended the sick. They buried the dead. They even had babies.

Farther and farther west they went. They could travel about 25 miles a day. When they entered Indian country, the wagons stayed close together for safety. Sometimes the Indians attacked these newcomers. But usually the Indians let them through.

Mountains were hard on the wagons. Broken wheels had to be fixed. Families with wrecked wagons had to crowd into other wagons. The 2,000-mile trip took about four months. Not everyone survived. Those who did had reached "the end of the trail" — Oregon.

Dr. Whitman worked hard to bring American farmers into Oregon. He even went back to Missouri to travel with one wagon train. Dr. McLoughlin also helped the American settlers. He sent food and guides to help them when they neared Oregon. Between 1840 and 1860 about 50,000 Americans arrived in Oregon. People wanted to go there very badly. It was said that they had "Oregon Fever."

Once in Oregon, the settlers cut down trees and built wooden houses. Many planted wheat. Some fished. Shopkeepers arrived in the wagon trains, too. They built stores. Towns grew. Portland, Salem (SAY • lehm), Corvallis (kore • VAL • ihs), and Oregon City were four towns begun by the 1840s.

State capitol mural shows settlers gathering in 1843 to decide whether Oregon Territory would be governed by America or Canada.

There were many more Americans than English people in Oregon. In 1846 the United States took control of the area. Oregon wasn't a state yet. In 1848 Oregon became a territory. It was land owned by the United States. At this time the Oregon Territory was very large. Today's states of Oregon, Washington, and Idaho (EYE • dah • ho), plus parts of Montana (mahn • TAN • ah) and Wyoming, were part of the Oregon Territory.

In 1848 gold was found in California. This helped the growth of the Oregon Territory. Some Oregon people went south and struck it rich. Others sold goods to people headed for the gold fields. Most people found little or no gold in California. But they heard that there was a treasure in the Oregon Territory. The treasure was fine farmland.

To help settle the Oregon Territory, the United States passed a law in 1850. It was called the Donation Land

Oregon's "treasure" was fine farmland.

Law. The law stated that a man who settled in Oregon before December of that year would get 320 acres of free land. His wife would also get 320 free acres. Suddenly, the few women in the Oregon Territory were like gold. Men searched for wives to get those 640 free acres.

Thousands of white settlers arrived. Indians lost their lands. Many grew angry. Indians had been pushed farther and farther west by American settlers. In Oregon, they could go no farther. They were backed up near the ocean.

Some Indians fought. Dr. Marcus Whitman and his wife were killed by Indians. This was near where Walla Walla, Washington is today. For revenge, Indian villages were destroyed in what is called the Cayuse (KYE • yoos) War.

This was a sad, bloody time. Settlers kept guns by their doorways in case of Indian raids. Indians never knew when white people might come to destroy their villages.

In 1855, white settlers murdered a number of Indians in Oregon's Rogue (ROHG) River Valley. This happened during what are known as the Rogue River Wars. The Rogue River Wars ended in 1856. That was when the Indians' leader, Chief John, surrendered. Chief John was put in prison.

By this time there were many settlers in Oregon. Fighting was over for a while. Oregon was getting ready to become a state. At this time Americans were arguing over slavery. Would Oregon allow slavery? Oregon people voted. They decided that Oregon would have no slavery. After this, the United States allowed Oregon to become a state. On February 14, 1859, Oregon became the thirty-third state. The little town of Salem was the capital. Millions of beavers had once lived in Oregon. It became known as the *Beaver State*.

The Indians were not finished fighting for their lands. White settlers tried to force the Modoc Indians onto a small piece of land. This land was known as a

A mural in the Oregon Senate chambers shows Oregon people on the day of statehood, February 14, 1859.

reservation. The Indians refused to go there. Their leader was a brave man named Kintpuash. He was called "Captain Jack." Captain Jack led his people into California. There, only 50 Indians held off 1,000 United States soldiers for a long while. "I do not want to fight," said Captain Jack. He asked for a home for his people on the Lost River, in Oregon. The government refused. Captain Jack then killed a United States general. Captain Jack was captured and hanged. His people were sent out of Oregon. In 1909 the Modocs were allowed to return. There were only 51 of them left.

One of the last battles was fought by the Nez Percé. They lived in northeastern Oregon. The Nez Percé were the first to breed Appaloosas (app • uh • LOO • suhz). These were spotted horses. The Indians loved to ride through their valley. These peaceful people had helped Lewis and Clark. But now gold was found on Nez Percé land. They, too, were told to go live on a reservation.

Soldiers forced the Nez Percé out of their valley. The Indians began to fight back. For 1,300 miles United States soldiers chased them toward Canada. The Indians fought the soldiers all along the way. Finally, the Nez Percé had to give up. Chief Joseph, their leader, said:

"I am tired of fighting. Our chiefs are killed. It is cold and we have no blankets. The little children are freezing to death. My heart is sick and sad. From where the sun now stands I will fight no more forever."

Some of the remaining Nez Percé were sent back to an Oregon reservation. By 1878 the Indian Wars in Oregon were over.

Chief Joseph of the Nez Percé surrendering in 1877

Today, only about 13,000 Indians live in the whole state of Oregon.

By 1883 train tracks ran all the way across the country. Traveling to Portland by train was a lot easier than traveling by covered wagon. In 1880 Oregon's population was about 175,000. By 1890 it had jumped to about 318,000. Portland grew into Oregon's biggest city. Lumber and farm products were processed there.

In the 1890s lumbering became big business in Oregon. Men called *lumberjacks* cut down the trees. "Timber!" they yelled. Douglas firs and pine trees fell. The trees were cut into logs. Often, the logs were floated down rivers to sawmills. At the sawmills, they were cut into lumber.

By 1938 Oregon was the leading lumber state. But in the early 1900s Oregon people had to learn some lessons about their forests. Lumber companies had cut down whole forests. They hadn't planted new ones. Laws were passed to protect forests. Today, new trees are planted when old ones are cut down. Insects also destroyed trees. Sprays were made to protect trees from insects. Fires have always been a great enemy of Oregon forests. One huge fire in 1933 destroyed millions of trees. Today, forest rangers watch for fires. "Smoke jumpers" parachute into forests to fight fires.

Douglas firs like these make up the largest part of Oregon's forests.

Today, Oregon is the number one lumber-producing state. Houses, furniture, paper, and many other products are made from Oregon lumber.

Lumber helped make Oregon a good place for shipbuilding. The ocean made it a good place to launch the ships. During World War I (1914-1918) ships were built in Portland and other shipyards. During World War II (1939-1945) warships and cargo ships were built. Supplies were shipped from Portland. They went to United States troops in the Pacific.

The fishing business also grew during the 1900s. Tuna has become the main fishing catch. Salmon are also caught in large numbers. Fish are packed in Astoria and other Oregon cities. Then they are sent to other cities in America.

Over the years, Oregon farmers had problems. Rivers flooded farms in some years. At other times, some areas didn't have enough water. Dams helped solve these problems. The Bonneville (BAHN • uh • vil) Dam was built in the 1930s. More dams were built in the 1960s and 1970s. These dams keep water from flooding farms. They release water to thirsty land in times of dry weather. The dams also turn water power into electricity.

Today, Oregon has much more than forests, fishing, and farming. It has a wide variety of animal life. Beautiful scenery brings thousands to see the state every year. But in recent years Oregon has had a problem with pollution. The air is not as clear as it used to be. The water is not as clean as it used to be. In the 1960s and

Oregon has a wide variety of wildlife. This painting shows a large number of waterfowl at the Tule Lake National Wildlife Refuge.

1970s lawmakers worked on pollution problems. They are hoping that Oregon will always be one of our most beautiful states.

You have learned about some of Oregon's history. Now it is time for a trip—in words and pictures—through the Beaver State.

Oregon is a Pacific Coast state. The Pacific Ocean touches its western edge. The state of Washington is to the north. Idaho is to the east. Nevada and California are to the south.

Pretend you are in an airplane high above Oregon. You pass over farms, forests, rivers, and valleys. Mountain ranges seem to reach up to your airplane. The Cascade Mountains go down the state. From a plane this mountain range looks almost like a backbone. The area east of the Cascades is sometimes called eastern Oregon. Here there are many wheat and cattle ranches. The area west of the Cascades is called western Oregon. Here lie the bigger cities and forests.

Pretend your airplane is landing in a big city in northwest Oregon. This is Portland. It is Oregon's largest city — by far.

Portland lies near the Columbia and Willamette rivers. Once, Chinook Indians fished for salmon in this area. Lewis and Clark explored here in 1806. A few years

Portland, with Mount Hood in the background

later, fur trappers and farmers settled here. By 1845 there were enough families to form a town.

Portland is nicknamed the *City of Roses.* Roses grow well where it is warm and wet. Portland is perfect for roses. There are many places where you can see lovely flower gardens. The International Rose Test Gardens and the Sunken Rose Gardens are two of the best.

The International Rose Test Gardens in Portland

The City of Roses has much that is beautiful. Mount Hood can be seen to the east. Forest Park is a huge, lovely woodland within the city.

The city has interesting museums. At the Portland Art Museum you can see Indian artwork. At the Oregon Historical Society you can learn about the history of the state. You can walk inside a giant model of your heart at the Oregon Museum of Science and Industry.

Visit the Washington Park Zoo in Portland. It is known for its elephant herd. If you like music, go to the Civic Auditorium. The Oregon Symphony Orchestra (SIM • foe • nee OHR • kess • trah) plays there. If you like basketball, go to the Memorial Coliseum. The Portland Trail Blazers play there.

The people of Portland work at many jobs. Portland is the state's main manufacturing city. Lumber is brought in from nearby forests. It is made into furniture and other wood products. Portland is at the northern edge of the Willamette Valley. That is an important farming area. Farmers send vegetables and fruits to Portland. There they are packaged. Many metal products are also made in Portland. Products go in and out of Portland by ship. The ships enter and leave the Port of Portland.

You remember John McLoughlin. McLoughlin founded Oregon City. That is a town just southeast of Portland. You can go inside Dr. McLoughlin's house there.

The state capitol building in Salem

Salem is about 50 miles south of Portland. Salem is the capital of Oregon. The city lies on the Willamette River.

Visit the state capitol building in Salem. A 24-foot-tall statue of a pioneer tops the state capitol building. Outside the building is a sculpture of a family on the Oregon Trail. Paintings of explorers Lewis and Clark can be seen inside.

Salem is not only the capital. It is also the state's third largest city. Millions of cans of fruits and vegetables are produced in Salem each year. Wood products, including paper, are also made there.

After seeing Salem, head west. You will be going toward the Pacific Ocean. When you get there, go south along the coast. You will see fishing boats going out onto the ocean. You will see lighthouses that guide boats to shore. The rocky shore is dangerous for ships. The stormy weather of the coast makes it even more dangerous. Many wrecked ships lie under the coastal waters.

At Cape Kiwanda it is easy to see why the rocky coast of Oregon is dangerous for ships.

Sunset at Bandon, on the Oregon coast

Interesting animals live near the shore. There are sea birds, such as sea gulls and sea parrots. Whales can be seen floating off the shore. Seals sun themselves on offshore rocks. Sea lions (a kind of seal) also live by the shore.

Visit Sea Lion Caves near Florence. These are the largest sea caves in the world. Sea lions live inside the caves between fall and spring. You can see baby sea lions sliding from the rocks into the water. One day each spring, all the sea lions slide off the rocks. They begin the long swim to their summer home in Alaska.

Take time from your trip down the coast to go inland a few miles. Visit Eugene. Once, Calapooya (kah • lah • POO • yah) Indians lived in this area. A settler named Eugene F. Skinner built a log cabin here in 1846. The town that grew here was named for him. Today, Eugene is Oregon's second biggest city.

Eugene lies at the south end of the Willamette Valley. Fruits and vegetables are grown in the area. They are sent to Eugene for packaging. Truckloads of lumber are brought to Eugene. There they are made into wood products.

You will see a lot of young people in Eugene. The city is the main home of the University of Oregon. You can visit museums at the University. At the Natural History Museum you can learn about minerals. At the Museum of Art you can see many fine paintings.

Eugene has a smaller "sister city" next to it. This is Springfield. It is a center for making wood products. Doors, fences, and plywood are made there.

In Springfield factories you can see how wood products are made. In years past, much lumber was wasted. Today, even sawdust is used. Some of it goes into insulation. That is what keeps buildings warm.

After visiting Eugene and Springfield, head back to the coast. You may notice the quick change in weather in this area. It can go from warm and sunny to cool and rainy in a short time. The coast of Oregon gets a lot of rain. In some years over 100 inches falls. "We don't get sunburned," say Oregon people who live near the coast. "We get rusted!"

Follow the coast southward. You will come to Oregon Dunes National Recreational Area. Some of the biggest sand dunes in the world are here.

Just south of the sand dunes you will come to the town of Coos (KOOSE) Bay. Coos Bay is one of the biggest ports in the world for shipping lumber to other places.

Petrified Gardens
at the Oregon Caves
National Monument

After traveling down the Oregon coast, swing east. Go across the lower part of Oregon. About 50 miles from the ocean you will come to Oregon Caves National Monument. Water and chemicals helped carve these caves. They were carved out of Elijah (ee • LYE • jah) Mountain. Inside the caves there are strange rock formations. Some of them look like icicles and draperies.

The city of Medford is very near the Oregon Caves. Medford was built when a railroad arrived in the area in 1883. The city lies in the Rogue River Valley. That is where Indian wars were once fought. Today, area farmers grow pears and apples. Medford is another Oregon lumbering town.

You have read a lot about lumber. Now it's time to find out where it comes from. Northeast of Medford is a huge forest area. Many kinds of trees can be found in Oregon's forests. Douglas firs grow there. They are among the biggest trees in the world. Some have grown over 380 feet tall. That's as tall as a 30-story skyscraper. Douglas firs are Oregon's main trees for lumber. Pine, cedar, and spruce trees also grow in Oregon. The state is said to have enough trees to rebuild every house in the United States. But Oregonians would never let that many trees be cut down. In some areas no tree cutting is allowed. People—and animals—enjoy such wilderness areas.

There are many animals in Oregon's forests and mountains. Deer live in the woodlands. Elk and pronghorn antelope roam through the state. Bobcats prowl through the mountains. Beavers gave the state its nickname. Once they were killed in huge numbers by fur trappers. Now they are protected. Beavers can be found in Oregon streams. A few timber wolves live in the

Snow rings Crater Lake in winter (above).
Phantom Ship (left) is one of the tiny volcanic
islands in Crater Lake.

forests. Coyotes, porcupines, and foxes are other wild

animals in Oregon. Pelicans can be seen at Upper

Klamath (CLAM • uth) Lake.

Oregon has one of the world's most beautiful lakes. It

is in a forested area about 60 miles northeast of Medford.

It is called Crater Lake.

You know that the lake was formed after the top of a volcano caved in. Water filled the hole. Crater Lake is about 1,932 feet deep. It is the deepest lake in the United States. Now it is part of Crater Lake National Park. People like to camp in the area.

Head northeast from Crater Lake. Go about 170 miles. You will come to the John Day Fossil Beds. Fossils of tiny camels have been found here. Bones of horses have also been found. Those horses were no bigger than dogs. They lived in Oregon many thousands of years ago.

Picture Gorge is near the Fossil Beds. This is a canyon. It was cut by the John Day River. Indians of long ago made pictures on the walls of the gorge.

After seeing Picture Gorge, head into eastern Oregon. There are more flat grasslands in eastern Oregon than in the west. You will see cattle grazing on the grasslands. Cowboys watch over them. The cattle are made into beef. Hogs and sheep are also raised in eastern Oregon.

The main farm product in the east—and the whole state—is wheat. The wheat is used to make bread, cakes, and breakfast cereals.

Eastern Oregon has no cities as big as Portland or Eugene. But Baker, La Grange, and Pendleton are three eastern cities. Farmers send their farm products to these cities.

Swing northwest of Pendleton. Follow the Columbia River along the state's northern border. It took thousands of years for the river to cut its way through the Cascade Mountains. The cut the river made through the mountains is called the Columbia River Gorge.

A rainbow shines over the Columbia River Gorge.

Multnomah Falls on the Columbia River Highway

You will see beautiful waterfalls on the Columbia River. There are also a number of dams on the river.

You will enjoy a visit to Bonneville Dam. You've seen ladders that people climb. Bonneville Dam has "fish ladders." They were built for the salmon.

Salmon are born in streams. When they are grown, they swim to the ocean. One day, they know it is time for them to produce their babies. They want to have them in the streams where they were born. The salmon try to get back to those streams. This instinct is very strong. They

Mount Hood. Trillium Lake is in the foreground.

leap over waterfalls. They swim against strong currents.
But there was no way for them to swim over huge dams.
That is why the "fish ladders" were built on Bonneville
Dam. The salmon can flip their way up the ladders.
Then they can finish their trip to their home streams.

To finish your own Oregon trip, head southeast. Go
about 20 miles from Bonneville Dam. You will come to
Mount Hood. The state has a number of very tall
mountains. Mount Hood is the tallest. It rises over two
miles high above the level of the ocean.

Mount Hood was once an active volcano. Fiery rock and gas erupted from its crater. It has been quiet in recent years. But at times smoke still comes out of the crater.

In the winter, people ski down Mount Hood. The top of Mount Hood is covered with snow—even in the summer. That is because it is always very cold that high on the mountain. You can hike to the top of Mount Hood. On the way you will see large areas of ice. They are known as *glaciers* (GLAY • shurz). Look down from the peak. You will know that you are looking at one of our most beautiful states.

A land of snow-covered mountains . . . roaring rivers . . . vast forests . . . and a long ocean shore.

Home to Indians . . . fur traders . . . lumberjacks . . . and fishermen.

Now a modern state with the big city of Portland.

The biggest lumber-producing state.

This is Oregon—the Beaver State.

Facts About OREGON

Area—96,981 square miles (10th biggest state)

Greatest Distance North to South—295 miles

Greatest Distance East to West—375 miles

Border States—Washington on the north; Idaho on the east; Nevada and California on the south; (the Pacific Ocean is to the west)

Highest Point—11,235 feet above sea level (Mount Hood)

Lowest Point—Sea level, on the shore of the Pacific Ocean

Hottest Recorded Temperature—119° F. (at Prineville on July 29, 1898, and also at Pendleton on August 10 of the same year)

Coldest Recorded Temperature—Minus 54° F. (at Ukiah on February 9, 1933, and also at Seneca on February 10 of the same year)

Statehood—Our 33rd state, on February 14, 1859

Origin of Name Oregon—The Columbia River was once called the *Ouragan*, a French word meaning *hurricane*. It is thought that the state's name came from this French word.

Capital—Salem

Earlier Capitals—Oregon City, Salem, and Corvallis (all while Oregon was still a territory)

Counties—36

U.S. Senators—2

U.S. Representatives—4

Electoral Votes—6

State Senators—30

State Representatives—60

State Song—"Oregon, My Oregon," by J.A. Buchanan and Henry B. Murtagh

State Motto—The Union

Nicknames—The Beaver State, the Pacific Wonderland, the End of the Trail

Fort Clatsop National Memorial

PORTLAND

Columbia River

WILLOWA WHITMAN NATIONAL FOREST

Three Arch Rocks National Wildlife Refuge

MT. HOOD NATIONAL FOREST

Warm Springs Indian Reservation

BLUE MOUNTAINS

SIUSLAW NATIONAL FOREST

WILLAMETTE NATIONAL FOREST

Silver Creek

CRATER LAKE NATIONAL PARK

Oregon Islands National Wildlife Refuge

FREMONT NATIONAL FOREST

HART MOUNTAIN NATIONAL ANTELOPE RANGE

Oregon Caves National Monument

State Seal—Adopted in 1859

State Flag—Adopted in 1925

State Flower—Oregon grape

State Bird—Western meadowlark

State Animal—Beaver

State Fish—Chinook salmon

State Tree—Douglas fir

State Rock—Thunder egg

State Colors—Navy blue and gold

Some Rivers—Columbia, Snake, Coquille, Rogue, Umpqua, Willamette, John Day, Deschutes, McKenzie, Clackamas

Some Lakes—Crater (deepest in the United States), Abert, Crescent, Silver, Summer, Upper Klamath

Some Waterfalls—Multnomah, Silver Creek, Salt Creek, Horse Tail, Latourelle

Main Mountain Ranges—Cascade, Blue, Coast, Klamath, Siskiyou, Steens, Wallowa

National Park—Crater Lake National Park

National Forests—11 entirely in state; 4 others partly in state

State Parks—Over 230

Animals—Deer, elk, pronghorn antelopes, beavers, foxes, coyotes, minks, otters, timber wolves, black bears, porcupines, chipmunks, squirrels, rabbits, pack rats, seals, sea lions, garter snakes, Pacific bull snakes, rattlesnakes, western meadow larks, sea gulls, sea parrots, pelicans, herons, mountain quails, hawks, owls, ducks, geese, pheasants, many other kinds of birds

Fishing—Tuna, salmon, cod, crabs, oysters, shrimp, white sturgeon, halibut, herring, trout, perch, bass

Farm Products—Wheat, beef cattle, milk and other dairy products, potatoes, hay, peppermint, cranberries, beans, nuts, strawberries, hops, sugar beets, green peas, apples, pears, cherries, flower bulbs

Mining—Stone, gravel, nickel, gold, silver, mercury

Manufacturing Products—Lumber, many kinds of wood products, paper products, many kinds of food products, machinery, chemicals, aluminum

Population—2,376,000 (1977 estimate; 30th most populous state)

Major Cities—Portland	368,000	(all 1979 estimates)
Eugene	101,900	
Salem	85,500	
Corvallis	42,300	
Springfield	38,600	
Medford	36,200	

44

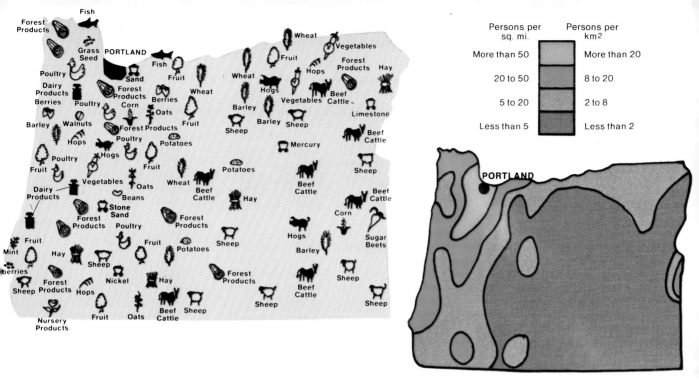

Oregon History

It is thought that there have been people in Oregon for over 10,000 years.

1543 — Bartolome Ferrelo, sailing for Spain, is thought to have explored the Oregon coast in this year

1579 — Englishman Sir Francis Drake is thought to have explored the coast

1778 — Englishman James Cook explores in area

1792 — American Robert Gray sails into a river and names it the Columbia after his ship

1805 — American explorers Lewis and Clark enter Oregon

1811 — Astoria, Oregon's oldest town, is begun as a fur-trading post by John Jacob Astor

1818 — United States and England agree that people of both countries can trade furs and farm in Oregon

1824 — John McLoughlin, the "Father of Oregon," arrives and rules fur-trading for England

1836 — Dr. Marcus Whitman travels on what will become the Oregon Trail; he establishes a mission in present-day Washington

1843 — A wagon train of about 120 wagons and 1,000 people travels on the Oregon Trail to Oregon

1845 — Portland is founded

1846 — United States takes control of the region by treaty with England

1847 — After Dr. Whitman and 13 others are killed by Indians at Walla Walla, settlers destroy Indian villages in Cayuse War

1848 — Oregon becomes a United States territory

1850 — Free land in Oregon as the Oregon Donation Land Law is passed!

1851-1856—Rogue River Indian Wars

1857—The "Father of Oregon," Dr. John McLoughlin, dies in Oregon City

1859—Oregon becomes the 33rd state on February 14; Salem is the capital

1860—Population of new state is 52,465

1861—Huge flood in the Willamette Valley; this same year the Civil War starts in the United States but there is no fighting in Oregon

1862—Eugene has become a city

1865—Civil War ends; this same year Mount Hood erupts

1868—Oregon State University is founded at Corvallis

1872-1873—Modoc Indian Wars; "Captain Jack" and Modoc Indians finally lose in California

1876—University of Oregon opens

1877—Nez Percé War ends as Chief Joseph surrenders in Montana

1878—Paiute and Bannock Indians are beaten at end of Indian fighting in Oregon

1883—Railroad reaches Portland; Medford is founded

1890—Thanks greatly to the railroad, the population of the state has increased to 317,704

1894—Fire at Silver Lake kills 40

1905—One hundred years after Lewis and Clark explored there, a world's fair called the Lewis and Clark Centennial Exposition is held in Portland

1912—Women gain the vote in Oregon

1914-1918—During World War I, 44,166 Oregonians fight for United States

1922—Astoria is almost destroyed by a fire; the city is rebuilt

1927—Schoolchildren pick western meadowlark as the state bird

1930—Population of state is 953,786

1935—State capitol building is burned in a fire

1937—Bonneville Dam is completed

1938—Oregon becomes the leading lumber-producing state (which it still is today)

1939—New state capitol building has been completed at Salem

1939-1945—During World War II, 147,633 Oregon men and women are in uniform; Oregon builds boats and sends supplies to army in the Pacific

1954—Linus Pauling, born in Portland, wins Nobel prize in chemistry

1959—Happy 100th birthday, Beaver State!

1962—Dr. Linus Pauling wins the Nobel peace prize

1964—Oregon is hit by the worst floods in the state's history

1967—Oregon is one of the first states to adopt the Federal Water Quality Act; the state is working on pollution problems

1970—Population of state is 2,091,385

1970s—More dams are built on the Columbia and Snake rivers

1975—Tualatin Project, which brings water to dry land, is completed

1977—Portland Trail Blazers are NBA champions!

1978—Victor Atiyeh is elected governor

46

INDEX

About the Author:

Dennis Fradin attended Northwestern University on a creative writing scholarship and graduated in 1967. While still at Northwestern, he published his first stories in *Ingenue* magazine and also won a prize in *Seventeen's* short story competition. A prolific writer, Dennis Fradin has been regularly publishing stories in such diverse places as *The Saturday Evening Post, Scholastic, National Humane Review, Midwest,* and *The Teaching Paper.* He has also scripted several educational films. Since 1970 he has taught second grade reading in a Chicago school—a rewarding job, which, the author says, "provides a captive audience on whom I test my children's stories." Married and the father of three children, Dennis Fradin spends his free time with his family or playing a myriad of sports and games with his childhood chums.

About the Artists:

Len Meents studied painting and drawing at Southern Illinois University and after graduation in 1969 he moved to Chicago. Mr. Meents works full time as a painter and illustrator. He and his wife and child currently make their home in LaGrange, Illinois.

Richard Wahl, graduate of the Art Center College of Design in Los Angeles, has illustrated a number of magazine articles and booklets. He is a skilled artist and photographer who advocates realistic interpretations of his subjects. He lives with his wife and two sons in Libertyville, Illinois.